Sojourn in Gascony

Pleasures of the Palette:
Sojourn in Gascony

Erasmus H. Kloman

Judd Publishing, Washington, D.C.

Designed by Kathy Klingaman Cunningham
Illustrations © Erasmus Helm Kloman
Copyright © 1994 by Judd Publishing, Inc.
All rights reserved
No part of this book may be reproduced without the written permission of the publisher.

Library of Congress Catalog Number 94-76957
Kloman, Erasmus Helm, 1921-
    Sojourn in Gascony, Pleasures of the Palette/Erasmus Helm Kloman
Illustrations by Erasmus Helm Kloman
1. Travel--France
2. Art--Painting
3. Cooking
ISBN 0-9639596-3-8

Published by Judd Publishing, Inc.
P.O.Box 40322, Washington, D.C. 20016

Table of Contents

Table of Illustrations   7
Table of Recipes   8
Acknowledgements   9
Foreword   11
Milestones in the History of Southwestern France   17
Week of October 5-11   25
    Lectoure
    Condom
    Hôtel de Bastard
    Musée Lapidaire, Lectoure
    La Romieu

Week of October 12-18   45
    Chateau d'Armagnac
    Fleurance
    Toulouse
    Larresingle
    Auch, Hôtel de France
    Fourcès
    Terraube, Le Vieux Perron

Week of October 19-25   63
    St. Clar
    Nérac
    Pau

    Francescas, Relais de la Hire
    Valence d'Agen
    Condom, Table des Cordeliers

Week of October 26-28   78
    Valençay, Hôtel Espagne
    Villandry
    Azay-le-Rideau
    Chinon
    Chateau Valençay
    Chateau Chambord

A Guide to Rental Housing in France   89

Table of Illustrations

Front cover
 Houses on Rue Fontélie, Lectoure

Front cover flap
 Maison de Retraite
 On a Clear Day You Can See the Pyrénées
 Larresingle
 Lectoure above the River Gers

Back cover
 Fourcès
 Nérac
 Round Hay Bales Near Lectoure
 Chateau de Villandry

Back cover flap
 Cathedral of St. Gervais-St. Portais
 Chateau Castelmore
 Chateau Chambord

Table of Recipes

Zucchini Soup   37

Stuffed Mussels and Billi Bi   40

Scallops Gascons   49

Onion Gratin with Gruyere Toasts   53

Lemon Souffle (sans flour)   58

Brie Sandwich (la fin/faim du monde)   59

Ratatouille Quiche   64

Rabbit Casserole Pruneaux   71

Herb Bread   73

Pâté   78

Acknowledgments

This book has been reviewed in various drafts by numerous friends and associates during a lengthy gestation. Indeed, so many readers have offered me encouragement and constructive criticism that just to list them all would make too long an introduction. I must, however, express my gratitude to a number of individuals whose insights and support have been crucial in seeing this endeavor through to a final product.

Without the keen judgment and patience of my wife the book would never have come into being. She has pointed out the hazards and helped navigate the course all the way while serving as editor of numerous drafts. Our dear friend Patricia Hass has reviewed several drafts while also advising on the mysteries of the world of publishing. Other friends who must be thanked include Alice Acheson, an esteemed artistic mentor, Luke Battle, who first encouraged me to publish, Ingrid Carlander, our literary landlady in Lectoure whose enthusiastic support has helped sustain my efforts, Henry Reuss, former U.S. Representative from Wisconsin, who with his wife Margaret, former chair of the Department of Economics at the

University of the District of Columbia, wrote The Unknown South of France, which was an invaluable resource in our travels in Gascony and in the writing of this book, and Burke Wilkinson, literary eminence grise of Washington and dispenser of invaluable advice.

Most of all I am indebted to Ruina (Rue) Judd, of Judd Publishing, whose contagious enthusiasm for this project has spurred me on. Recognizing a potential embedded in the manuscript she masterminded its transformation into a book and provided a niche on her company's list. Happily, she chose Lynne Shaner as editor, and for that choice I will always be grateful. Lynne's highly honed editorial skills proved indispensable, and it was my great privilege to work with her.

Foreword

For six of the nine Octobers since my retirement, Sue, my wife, and I have rented a house in some part of southern France. Each year we find a different house so that we can sample the great variety of venues in an area justly known for its natural beauty, wealth of ancient monuments, and culinary wonders, to mention only some of many attractions. The first several years we had rented homes in either Provence or the Côte d'Azur, but three years ago we ventured to the southwest and chose a house in Gascony in the town of Lectoure, the ancient capital of the Lomagne region. The area is mercifully untraveled by tourists, and we didn't encounter another foreigner. Travel guides, quite incorrectly in our judgment, rate few places in the area as more than mildly interesting, which may account in part for the scarcity of tourists in comparison with Provence, for example.

Lectoure and its surrounding countryside are little known even among the French outside the region. The province of Gascony is recognized today mainly as a center for production of Armagnac and *foie gras* and as the home of d'Artagnan, Captain of Musketeers serving King Louis XIV and immortalized by Alexandre Dumas in *The Three Musketeers*.

The historic roots of this province sink deep into the past, specifically to an invasion in 580-86 across the Pyrénées Mountains by a Spanish tribe, the Vascones, from which the name of Gascony is derived. The invaders successfully challenged the Roman occupiers of this territory. They even appointed national dukes against whom Charlemagne had to fight early in his reign. His Carolingian successors were finally able to establish their own dukedoms in the ninth century. During the feudal era, Gascon history fell into a confusing obscurity in which numerous counts, viscounts, and seigneurs contested for power. During the Hundred Years' War, Gascony became the battlefield for contending English and French forces. England retained predominant control until the French monarchs, aided by Joan of Arc, won Gascony back and incorporated it into France in the middle of the fifteenth century.

Contemporary Gascony is ringed by several more widely known areas including Bordeaux facing the Atlantic; Perigord and the Dordogne to the north; Languedoc to the southeast; and the Pays Basque to the southwest. Lest it be thought that Gascony resembles the proverbial hole in the doughnut, the truth is quite to the contrary. The Gascons, with their own strong sense of regional identity, have borrowed selectively from the cultures of their neighbors while stamping their own personality on all such adaptations.

Getting to know the distinguishing characteristics of various regions of France is one of the tremendous rewards of renting a house in the provinces. The value of these rewards can hardly be overstated, but they do not come without certain challenges. Despite all we have learned over the years we still find ourselves being surprised and sometimes dismayed by French bureaucracy and commonplace features of daily life that differ from what we're accustomed to at home. During our sojourn in Gascony all of Europe was experiencing exceptionally wet weather and we saw far less of the sun than we would have liked. But the sunlight seemed perhaps even more radiant when it did burst through. Learning to cope with the occasional vicissitudes is part of the adventure. Thus we keep going back, and the good memories replace recollections of the times when things fell apart.

Sue and I are lucky in many ways. Since my retirement, I have pursued a second career as an artist and I find endless inspiration in France. Aside from her keen interest in gardening, Sue's creative talents lie mainly in the culinary arts. She is a serious cook who appreciates everything to do with cuisine from the cultivation of the land, through the marketing of the produce, to the preparation of the dishes served at the table. Together we observe our surroundings through the artist's eye while tasting the regional specialties of the places we visit with the appreciation of aspiring gourmets, managing thereby to enjoy the very best that France can offer.

Is there any place where the bond between good art and great food is more pronounced than in France? Think of all the still lifes of fruit, vegetables, wine, fish, game, and bread. Consider how nearly every French restaurant boasts an art collection and how the quality of the art usually correlates with the quality of the cooking. Recall how one of the great private collections of the Impressionists was amassed at the Colombe d'Or restaurant in St. Paul de Vence when impoverished artists paid their bills with paintings they could not sell. Though other national cuisines have gained favor in recent times and artistic creativity knows no national boundaries, France maintains its reputation as a standard setter in both arenas.

Gascon gastronomy is a combination of many influences—the strong spicy flavors of the mountains to the south,

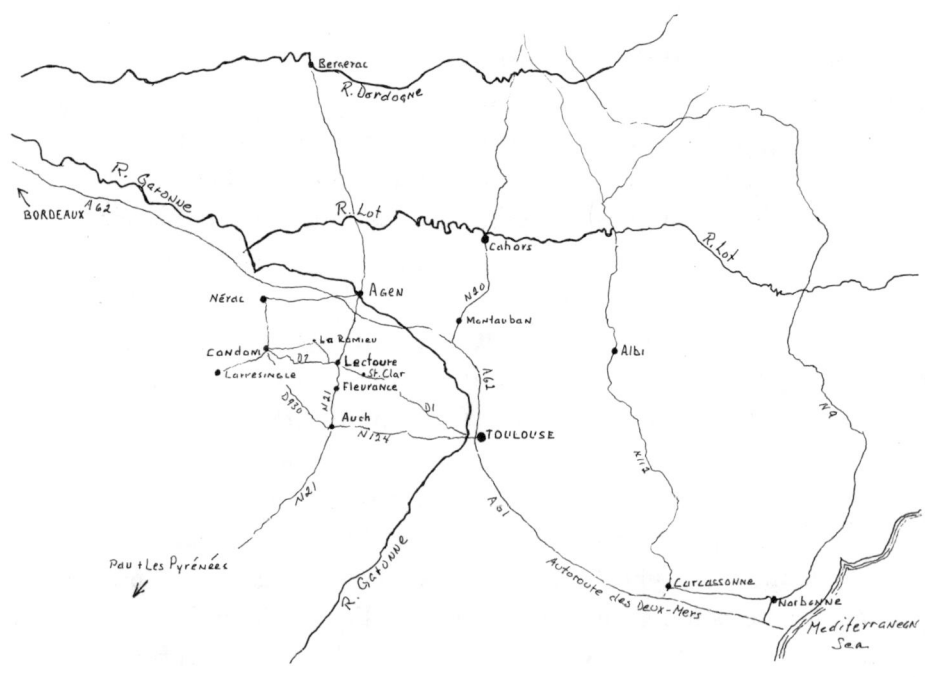

an adaptation of the elegant styles of Bordeaux and Perigord to the north, and always the rich and succulent traditional cuisine of the Armagnac region. The Gascons like hearty portions, and *nouvelle cuisine* has made only limited inroads on Gascon tables. In view of their exceptionally hearty diet and the small numbers of overwieght people one sees, Gascony appears to be a most convincing case for proving there is indeed a *"paradoxe français."*

Over the years we have developed a certain outlook that could be called a travel philosophy. We present it here as a point of view that might be helpful to other like-minded travelers. The guidelines of this philosophy are as follows:

1. Be adaptable. Life is more enjoyable abroad if one adapts to the customs of the local inhabitants.

2. Don't be afraid to try out your French. In recent years the French have been more receptive to foreigners' attempts to use their language, and in many smaller cities, few inhabitants understand English.

3. Avoid tourists and the tourist season. Most American and other foreign tourists flock to France in the summer.

4. Eschew the "notch in gun barrel" approach. How much more pleasurable to follow a more leisurely pace and to recall places where one has lingered instead of the blur of memories of places seen on the run!

5. Do not expect to be welcomed into neighboring households. The French reputation for admitting only family and

old friends into the privacy of their homes is well founded.

6. Live well for little. The cost of living in France tends to be high, but there are many ways to be thrifty. One of the greatest pleasures comes from visits to surrounding towns on their regular market days. Become skilled in the art of the picnic.

7. Make plans but stay loose. Although we enjoy doing advance research, we also take advantage of recommendations picked up in our daily contacts. Often we rely on sheer luck.

8. Invite friends or family to visit. Sharing your adventures with visitors will enhance your own enjoyment of these sojourns in places of unsurpassed natural beauty, where the past is a vital part of the present and where the pace of life slows to a leisurely amble.

Milestones in the History of Southwestern France

To acquaint the reader with the history of the region, following is a basic primer of some of the more important people, places, and dates cited in the narrative.

700,000 - 400,000 B.C.   *Homo erectus* appeared in Pyrenean foothills. Archaeological evidence in caves and rock shelters has been found widely scattered throughout Southwestern France.

100,000 - 30,000 B.C.   *Homo sapiens* Cro-Magnon, the first modern human, appeared. Bones and artifacts were found by archaeologists in Aurignac in 1869 and later at Les Eyzies on the Vézère, tributary of the Dordogne.

35,000 - 7,000 B.C.   Over these millennia, artists of the caves created their works in the Dordogne, Vézère, and Célé Valleys.

Circa 7,000 B.C.   The last European glaciers melted and this phase of the Ice Age ended.

6,000 - 2,000 B.C.	The Neolithic descendants of Cro-Magnon raised crops and domesticated animals.
700 - 500 B.C.	Celtic tribes from beyond Rhine penetrated the region.
Circa 600 B.C.	Greeks established a settlement in Massallia (Marseilles).
51 B.C. to 410 A.D.	Romans conquered all of Aquitaine (water land) in 28 B.C. The Pax Romana lasted about three centuries.
413 A.D.	The fall of Rome marked beginning of a six-century era of dark ages in southern France. In the absence of a governing authority anarchic forces were set loose.
405 - 475 A.D.	Visigoths, Burgundians, and Franks invaded the area.
496 A.D.	Clovis, Chief of a Frankish tribe, became the first ruler of the region to convert to Christianity.
507	The Franks drove the Visigoths south into Spain and seized Aquitaine, which eventually evolved into the French nation.
768 - 814	Charlemagne built an empire based on the Roman model. He was crowned Holy

Roman Emperor by Pope Leo III in 800. According to legend the aging emperor ordered construction of the shrine of St. Jacques (St. James) of Compostela after the Saint appeared to him in a dream. Charlemagne also ordered the Saint's remains to be brought back to churches along the Compostela trail, which in later centuries, was traversed by pilgrims from all parts of Europe.

1000 - 1300 This is the period known as the High Middle Ages. The Church became a great unifying force. Cistercian, Franciscan and Dominican monastic orders were established.

1137 Eleanor of Aquitaine, ruler of entire Duchy of Aquitaine including Gascony, married Louis VII of France. After divorcing him in 1152, she married Henry Plantagenet of Anjou who inherited the crown of England. They chose to rule their vast domain from Poitiers, the site of their court in Aquitaine. After Henry's death in 1189, Eleanor ruled alone until ceding the crown to her eldest son, Richard I in 1199. Poetry, arts, and songs of the troubadours flourished in Eleanor's court.

1152 - 1453 B.C. A period of war between the English and the French culminated in the Hundred

Years' War. English power was centered on Bordeaux while the French generally controlled the territories surrounding Aquitaine. The French and English built over 1000 fortified towns, *(bastides)*, most of which remain standing throughout the region.

1209 - 1229   The French King and the Pope launched the Albigensian Crusade against the Cathar heresy, which was centered in the town of Albi. After losing this struggle the counts of Toulouse submitted nominally to the sovereignty of French King.

1309 - 1377   The papacy was moved from Rome to Avignon.

1360   In the treaty of Bretigny, King Edward III of England renounced claim to the French throne while being ceded new lands in Aquitaine. The bubonic plague ravaged Europe.

1453 - 1562   The era of the Renaissance witnessed a strong Italian influence on French architecture and the arts. Fortress castles became increasingly obsolete with the perfection of siege artillery. Renaissance chateaux were built to accommodate life styles of noble families.

1473   Forces of French King Louis XI defeated the tyranical Jean V, last of the counts of Armagnac in Lectoure.

1527   Marguerite d'Angoulême (Margaret of Navarre), sister of French King François I, married Henri d'Albret. Their court in Nérac became a center of literary and artistic development. This court also fostered religious reform culminating in strong Protestant opposition to Catholicism.

1562 - 1610   During the Religious Wars, France was torn apart by bitter conflict between Catholics and Protestants. St. Bartholomew's Day Massacre of Huguenots occurred in 1572.

1572   Henri d'Albret's grandson, also named Henri, married Marguerite de Valois, sister of the French King. On coming into line to ascend the French throne as Henri IV, he forsook his Protestant belief, saying "Paris is worth a mass." A ladies' man of remarkable prowess, Henri came to be known fondly as Le Vert Galant.

1598   Henri IV issued the Edict of Nantes, which guaranteed freedom of religion for Protestants.

1610 Henri IV was assassinated, and the persecution of Protestants resumed.

1685 Louis XIV revoked the Edict of Nantes, precipitating a mass emigration of Huguenots. A brutally enforced national unification program to bring Aquitaine into the mainstream of French life was begun.

1715 The death of Louis XIV marked the beginning of an age of forward-looking administrators in the provinces and the rebuilding of towns in the southwest.

1789 - 1804 French Revolution followed by era of turbulence leading to rise of Napoleon and his coronation in 1804. After the revolution, the southwestern region remained more fervently committed to the original revolutionary objectives: Liberté, Egalité, Fraternité.

For the last two centuries the history of southwestern France has been linked with that of the French nation. Since most of the historical events cited in the following pages occurred before the revolution, this chronology covers only the more distant past.

This account is based largely on *Sue's* daily diary, on which I have elaborated to provide a historical and geographical context. An annotated list of directories and other sources for rental houses appears at the back of the book for readers who may wish to seek the same pleasures we have found.

Lectoure

Sojourn in Gascony

Week of October 5-11

Monday & Tuesday

We flew from Washington via New York to Paris, then on by Air Inter to Toulouse. We leased a car and started to Lectoure, delighted with the views of verdant countryside, every inch of which was carefully cultivated.

The house in Lectoure had been recommended to us by an old friend. Through him we contacted the owner, a Parisian journalist who sent us photos and literature on the house and town of Lectoure. Her daughter, Astrid, lives there year round, staying in one wing when the main part of the house is rented.

Leasing the cart at the airport and finding our way from the airport to the road to Lectoure proved a challenge. Then finding our house in a strange town was another hurdle. But we did find it, met Astrid, and moved into our quarters. The house, dating from 1798, is commodious and comfortable and overlooks about an acre of terraced gardens mostly suggesting a certain insouciance in upkeep. The top terrace offers a spectacular view of the rich farmland stretching some sixty miles south to the Pyrénées.

While the front of the house looks out on the garden and the view below, the back faces directly on a street. To the left of the tall three-floor main section is an elongated one-storey wing containing utilities, storage, and at the far end, Astrid's living quarters. The main sitting room or salon is entered directly from the garden patio. It is the most welcoming space at this level, being furnished with an eclectic assortment of antiques and modern pieces, a wall lined with well-stocked bookshelves, and a huge raised fireplace. Other rooms on the ground floor include a tiny but well-equipped kitchen, a capacious and somewhat formal dining room, and a large guest suite.

From the back of the sitting room a long flight of stairs leads to the second floor, where an enormous master bedroom and smaller guest room are located. One bath serves both. In the master bedroom a very long row of closets (rare for French households), huge double bed, and high casement windows overlooking the garden provide great comfort, convenience, and aesthetic rewards.

Our first day had not been entirely hassle-free. In addition to the travel-related stress, we had been greatly disappointed in the low standards of the supermarket we had visited to stock up on a few basic staples. But even so, as the day drew to a close, we were blissfully content to set our dinner table by the fire and begin plotting our excursions for the weeks ahead. In Washington we had read whatever we could find about our new surroundings. By far the best account in English was *The Unknown South of France* (Harvard Common Press, 1991) by Henry and Margaret Reuss, a lively guide to the history of the area with invaluable advice on inns, restaurants and other amenities. Later we found an excellent guidebook, *South West France, Aquitaine, Gascony, the Pyrénées* by Andrew Sanger, (Passports Regional Guides of France, 1990). We also relied heavily on both *Guides Michelin* (Pneu Michelin, 1993)—the green for regional background and the red for restaurant advice.

Wednesday

We savored every morsel of our first morning breakfast, typically French in its simplicity. Starting with fresh orange juice (Sue refuses to serve anything from a jar or a carton), we also enjoyed triple strength coffee (for her one and only cup of the day, Sue insists on a strong brew), a baguette, sweet butter, and Bonne Maman marmalade.

After breakfast we took our first walk into town, a short uphill climb, only three minutes from our house to the main street.

We were relieved to find two good supermarkets, and a variety of smaller shops and a newspaper dealer who carried the *Herald Tribune*, though alas it arrives a day late in Lectoure.

In the coming days we gradually got to know Lectoure. Begun in the Gallo-Roman era around the first century, A.D. on the lowlands, the town was relocated on its present high promontory to allow easier defense against invasions. Most of the ramparts remain intact. At the eastern end of town is the ruin of the chateau of the counts of Armagnac, looking out on the valley of the Gers River. In the center of town is the thirteenth-century Gothic church of Saint Gervais. Once boasting the designation of Cathedral, this church was joined to its neighbor, St. Protais, in an architectural amalgam mixing two very different styles. Built on the site of a Roman temple that itself replaced an important Celtic religious site, the structure suffered severe damage in 1473 when troops of Louis XI stormed the town and defeated the forces of the Count D'Armagnac thus bringing to an end the independence of the Armagnac region. The church was further damaged during the religious wars of the sixteenth century.

Still settling in on our second day, we cut short our initial survey of Lectoure to visit the market, open weekly in Condom, the town closest to Lectoure. Needless to say the town has become the butt of many jokes, but it benefits greatly from an influx of tourists who buy large numbers of postcards and other souvenirs and have themselves photographed next to the town signposts and especially at the palace of the bishops of Condom. In fact, the device, usually called a *préservatif* by the French, was invented some 400 years ago by Jean Condom, but it is not known whether he ever lived in the town bearing his name. The townspeople have learned to rise above the snickering of tourists, while happily pocketing the francs the town's unusual name brings.

Old wealth from vineyards, especially those used to produce grapes for Armagnac, is reflected in the streets lined with handsome private residences. One row of imposing townhouses, very formal and sophisticated, in the manner of the late eighteenth and early nineteenth centuries, faces a tree-lined park. A sixteenth-century Gascon gothic cathedral with a cloister of later vintage and an Armagnac museum are visitor attractions.

Condom is an outstanding example of how a provincial

town can assure the preservation of a community's historic heritage. The townspeople, their leaders, and the local *Syndicat d' Initiative* (Chamber of Commerce) work together to nurture civic awareness of important monuments, buildings, and regional traditions. Fortunately, both the town of Condom and the surrounding countryside have much to sustain their economic viability in the way of viticulture, production of *foie gras*, and the facilities to attract tourists.

We were somewhat thwarted on our fist day of serious marketing when we found that most of the stalls in the Condom market were closing down as we arrived. (Ordinarily, Sue buys a roasting chicken at the start of our stay. Easy to cook, a good size chicken can be the basis for several meals before winding up as chicken stock.) However, we did find both a farm produce vendor and a cheese and olive vendor. When we told the vegetable lady that we had arrived too late to buy a roasting chicken, she sold us the one she had bought for herself. We were most grateful, but once back in our kitchen, Sue found that neither the head nor the feet had been severed, and that unwelcome chopping task fell to her. Adhering to local tradition, Sue put these parts to good use in making chicken stock.

One of the first tasks we perform on settling into a new location is to make a list of the market days in our own and neighboring towns. Although many farmers and vendors move their wares regularly from one market to another within their region, each market has an individual character.

Markets vary in size. Food products are, of course, the feature attraction, and the food stalls offer a staggering variety of fresh farm produce, locally produced cheese, numerous types of olives, highly spiced sausages encrusted with local herbs (a staple of Gascon fare), fish, meat, and game. A wide range of household goods, especially kitchen ware, is presented along with clothing, garden items, pet supplies, and barnyard animals. While it is possible to buy the same items in supermarkets or smaller specialty shops, indoor stores lack the appealing atmosphere of outdoor markets.

Sue's practicality and thrift, for which I often tease her, are ideally suited to shopping in these markets and managing a household in France. She regards most potential problems as challenges to her ingenuity. This Robinson Crusoe attitude has often stood us in good stead.

After our marketing we went home for lunch. Astrid came by for an aperitif before dinner. With her came Tequila, her ancient German Shepherd.

Thursday

Today we had mostly sunny weather, doubly pleasing because we were to meet Sue's daughter Laura at Toulouse airport. We took a lovely meandering road, called the D-7, and had no trouble reaching the airport and meeting Laura's flight. When we got back to Lectoure it was sunny enough to have a late lunch on our little terrace.

While Laura caught up a bit on lost sleep, I sketched the Maison de Retraite, a lovely eighteenth-century building just on the other side of our entrance gate. Since our arrival I had been scouting for sketchable sites and had been particularly attracted to this one. The tiled roof and pale yellow stucco walls; arched windows with white shutters; and the central portal topped by the ironwork Virgin and trumpeting angels all beckoned. It was built originally as a Tannerie Royale and now provides an ideal setting as a home for the elderly. We were struck by how many younger people came to visit their relatives and the totally uninstitutional aspect of the complex. A far cry from most commercial retirement homes in the United States!

Seating myself on a low wall in front of the building, I made an initial sketch in ink backed up by Polaroid photos. Later, I revised the drawing and painted the first of several watercolors executed during our stay in Lectoure. Most of these pieces fall somewhere between rough sketches and finished works. I have depicted architecture, one of my favorite subjects, in most of the pieces.

For dinner that day we went to the Hôtel de Bastard, an elegant hostellerie recommended to us by friends who had stayed there while on a walking tour several years ago. Its restaurant served an excellent dinner at a quite reasonable price. The dining rooms and other ground floor salons are decorated in a deep, rich ocher color. Blue accents in the curtains, chairs, and china complete the scheme. Built in 1747 by a prominent military figure, François Dominique de Castaing, it was modeled on similar *hôtels particuliers* (large townhouses) in Condom. The builder, having no children, bequeathed his house to Baron Jean Baptiste de Bastard, head of another prominent local family well-connected throughout France. (The French find nothing odd about the name because their word for bastard is *bâtard*.) After several other transmutations the building was adapted to its present use in 1983. Today it is without rival in the Lectoure area for its cuisine and the appeal of its ambiance.

Like most restaurants in Gascony, the Hôtel de Bastard features mostly dishes based on *foie gras* (literally fat liver). In driving through the Gascon countryside one sees numerous large fields and barnyards of geese and ducks barely able to waddle because they are force-fed maize to produce the enlarged liver so highly prized by French gourmets. A common device on farms is a rounded stick, which is used to push the maize far enough into the goose's throat to activate the bird's swallowing mechanism. This causes the metabolism to malfunction and the liver to enlarge. The cruelty of this practice seems to have gone completely unnoticed by French animal rights activists.

The high-quality maize that is force-fed to geese and ducks to enlarge the liver makes the rest of the meat exceptionally tender and tasty while still remaining quite lean. The *magret* or breast of duck or goose served all over the Southwest is so succulent that it is only lightly cooked, sometimes emerging from the kitchen almost raw. These fowl, like the chickens, range freely in the farmyard thereby acquiring a taste far superior to mass-produced creatures sold in U.S. chains. (However, due to their obesity they do not range very far.)

A special regional delicacy is *confit*, a potted meat made of a duck or goose cooked and preserved in its own fat. However unappealing this may seem to the uninitiated, *confit* is an essential ingredient of Gascon cooking especially in enriching the stews, casseroles and cassoulets for which the region is famous. The dish best known outside of Gascony, of course, is *pâté de foie gras.* Invented in the eighteenth century by Chef Jean Joseph Close, who cooked the goose liver with truffles and served it under a pastry crust, (*en croute*).

The Hôtel de Bastard menu offers a range of wonderful choices aside from foie gras, some on the pricey side, while a more limited three-course meal at a modest price is a fine alternative. Optional with the latter is a carafe of a good red wine from the Côtes de Gascogne. House specialties include a flaky *feuilleté* (puff pastry) and a crispy vegetable *ragout* (stew). For dessert try either the *pastis*, an orange and brandy-flavored yeast cake traditionally made with goose fat but now more commonly with butter, or the apple- or prune-filled *croustade*, a deep pastry case soaked in Armagnac and topped with thin curling flakes of pastry, both regional specialties.

    I had immediately recognized the Hôtel de Bastard's architecture as an irresistible subject to paint. Its neoclassical lines, the rich cream-colored stone of its walls that set off the handsome eighteenth-century window and door frames in brilliant white, and the grill work of the facing courtyard were absolutely compelling. To bring the tower of the cathedral into the background my sketch took a bit of artistic license. I used a combination of raw and burnt sienna and Naples yellow to carry out the monochromatic treatment.

    Armagnac, a staple in the Hôtel de Bastard cuisine, is said to be France's oldest brandy. While the quality of different producers may vary considerably, an Armagnac properly matured in oak is extremely smooth, refined, and more flavorful than other brandies. A thin white wine produced from one of three strictly controlled grape varieties is mixed with eight other permitted grape types, distilled in a special pot still, and aged, first for two years in new oak barrels, and then for as long as twenty years in older barrels. Lectoure and Condom are in the northern sector of the prosperous Armagnac region whose soil and climate are uniquely suited to the production of this *eau de vie*.

    Over our three-week stay we also developed a keen appreciation for many local wines, which are strong tasting and well suited to the spicy dishes of the region. Madiran, a potent full-bodied red from an area below Armagnac, became our favorite. Pacherenc du Vic Bilh, with its unpronounceable name, is a good white, although a trifle sweet for our taste. The Vins de Béarn, from vineyards to the south, include an excellent rosé.

On leaving the hotel to walk home after dinner we agreed that the Bastard's cuisine and ambiance deserved a return visit. We met a friendly alley cat whom we had first encountered on our way into dinner. He was checking out trash containers that had been left on the sidewalk.

Friday

Weather reverted to clouds and rain after yesterday's partially sunny spell. We walked to the marché in Lectoure, which is spread out on either side of the main street. Markets in Lectoure are held regularly on Fridays regardless of weather conditions. Laura bought one of the superb local melons, some delicious tiny mussels and the makings of a great salad—mache, arugula, lettuce and artichokes. Sue stocked up on cheese, ham (jambon de Bayonne), and mushrooms.

Even though Sue does not like goat cheese, she knows that Laura and I do. Thus she included two small *beauforts*, along with a *tomme*, and a section of *Bethmale*, one of the local cheeses made from cow's milk. Bayonne ham is a wonderful addition to any picnic, with or without melon. Of the many types of wild mushroom we have come to prefer *cèpes*, the large *porcini* that appears during the spring and fall. Sue has also experimented with the apricot-colored *chanterelles*, and the morel. Though we have often had dishes featuring truffles at restaurants, they have been either too pricey or unavailable in markets we have visited.

In the afternoon we visited the Musée Lapidaire adjacent to St. Gervais. In 1540 the bishops discovered a remarkable collection of Mithraic bull sacrificial altars or *tauroboles*. The ancient Gauls of this area were among the last to convert to Christianity, and these votive stones were used in rites of the followers of Mother Cybele until the sixth century. Now they are in a labyrinth of a museum made from caverns that once housed the bishops' wines. The principal faces of the altars bear commemorative inscriptions, while the sides feature the head of a bull or ram and various cult objects, as shown in this illustration. One Celtic rite involved baptism with the blood of a bull to wash away sins. Mosaics of the Gallo-Roman era, vases, bronzes, coins, and a remarkable Pyrénées marble sarcophagus are also on display. There is also a deep well thought to have been used as a receptacle for cremated ashes in the fifth century.

The makers of the *tauroboles* and the other Gallo-Roman artifacts were the earliest artists whose works have survived in today's Lectoure. Since then, Lectoure has not been noted for artistic achievement, nor are the other towns in the surrounding region notable for well-known artists or art colonies. Indeed, it is the relative obscurity or undiscovered aspect of this corner of France that makes it so appealing.

We left the museum and walked into the adjoining park that looks out to the vast expanse of rolling terrain toward the Pyrénées about sixty-five miles to the south. Astrid told us that the mountains were visible only infrequently, and that, if they could be seen, rainy weather was likely to follow. During our three weeks stay we saw the mountains only once, and then they stood up in a startling display of snow-capped peaks high on the horizon. Astrid's prediction of rain to follow proved accurate.

Before leaving the park we picked up a few fallen branches to supplement our limited supply of firewood. Though the weather today was quite mild, on returning home we lit another fire to dispel the dampness and to enhance the atmosphere in our living room where we again had our dinner. Tonight we sampled a local rosé wine. First course was zucchini soup.

Sue always brings a few favorite recipes to France keeping in mind the availability of the ingredients in local markets.

Zucchini Soup

Ingredients:
3 teaspoon butter
3 lbs zucchini (washed & sliced)
1 large clove garlic (minced)
1/4 cup chopped shallots
1 1/4 cup warm chicken stock
1/2 cup sour cream
1/2 to 1 teaspoon curry powder
salt and pepper
minced parsley for garnish

Cook zucchini, garlic, shallots, and curry in butter covered over low heat until softened but not browned. Scrape into blender jar. Add stock, sour cream, salt and pepper. Blend 30 seconds or until zucchini is pureed. Chill. Stir before serving in chilled cups and garnish with parsley. Good hot also. Serves 4.

Saturday

We drove north to the caves in which the drawings of prehistoric peoples have been preserved over the centuries. We had given far too little attention to the route to be taken or the distances involved and thus allowed nowhere near enough time for what proved a very long trip. Our original goal was to visit the famous caves of Lascaux, although we knew that the real caves have been closed to the general public to protect against further environmental deterioration and that we would be able to see only the duplicate, Lascaux Deux. Our dilatory departure combined with a time-consuming detour and a couple of wrong turns forced us to redirect ourselves towards the Grotte du Pech Merle. This change in plans turned out for the best in every way.

Our tour guide never tired of boasting that these caves, discovered in 1922, had more to offer than Lascaux, discovered only in 1940. While we are not able to judge the relative merits of the two, we can certainly say that Pech Merle exceeded even our high expectations.

The winding drive first along the Lot and then on the Célé River goes through deep gorges cut over millennia by the rushing waters. Before entering the caves the visitor may visit an excellent museum about prehistoric times and see a film on Pech Merle. The tour itself passes through about fifteen underground galleries where the remarkably accurate and graceful paintings by Cro-Magnon humans are visible. Bison, bears, mammoths, horses, and human figures appear as if drawn only yesterday. Seeing these artworks, some of which date back to 18,000 BC, puts the viewer in awe of their creators. One tries to imagine how they came to penetrate the caverns so deeply, what motivated them to make these drawings, how they made the torches that lit the walls where they painted and how they discovered the art of painting and the materials to use.

One fascinating form repeated in several of the galleries is the outline of the human hand, a negative image presumably created by blowing or smearing a dark pigment on the hand and the area surrounding it. Such "signatures" are found in cave paintings in many other areas.

The echo of our guide's voice in the caves made it difficult to understand all he was saying. In pointing to the animal figures he referred often to *"les pattes avant,"* the forefeet or front paws. I was convinced he was saying *"les pantalons"* and asked Laura and Sue to explain why these prehistoric creatures were presumed to wear trousers. My question evoked unrestrained guffaws.

Taking a much shorter route than our circuitous drive to Pech Merle we arrived home in time to make a hearty dinner of stuffed mussels. We all agree that Mediterranean mussels have much more flavor than those we buy at home.

Stuffed Mussels

Ingredients:
2 quarts mussels
1 cup each of white wine and water
1 onion chopped
1 shallot chopped
1 tomato (peeled, seeded, and chopped)
1 T minced fresh basil
1/2 teaspoon tomato paste
salt and pepper,
2 T butter
1/4 cup stale breadcrumbs
Parmesan cheese
1 T olive oil or butter

Wash and remove "beards" from 2 quarts mussels. Steam them until shells open along with the chopped onion and shallot in wine and water. Discard any mussels with shells unopened. Strain and reserve liquid for making Billi Bi.

Shell mussels, separate shells, retaining half and place one mussel in each open shell.

Duxelles (filling): Sauté 1 tomato (peeled, seeded, and chopped) with 1 T minced fresh basil, 1/2 teaspoon tomato paste, salt and pepper, in 2 T butter for 10 minutes, or until liquid evaporates.

Add 1/4 cup stale breadcrumbs and salt and pepper. Remove from heat and mix well.

Cover each mussel with some of duxelle mixture. Arrange in shallow baking dish, sprinkle with

Parmesan cheese and oil or melted butter, bake in preheated oven 450° for 10 minutes or until topping is golden. Serve with lemon slices. Serves 4.

The reserved broth from the steaming of the mussels is used to make a delicious soup.

Billi Bi (mussel soup):

Reduce mussel liquid by half or until flavor is quite strong (from five to ten minutes). Add 1/2 cup of cream to each cup of broth and season with salt and pepper to taste. Garnish with parsley. Serve chilled or hot.

Sunday

Morning rain gave way to partial sunshine, which encouraged Sue and Laura to do the laundry and hang it out to dry on the lower terrace. We have found that doing the laundry with European washing machines is not a chore to be entered into casually, and our experience has been fraught with bother. The controls offer a vast array of choices for various ways to run the machine, but only a rocket scientist can fathom the instructions. Machines we have encountered take only very small loads that pass through many cycles of loud gurgling and churning separated by long rest periods. The whole process lasts an eternity.

Laggardly leaving laundry to the ladies, I took my usual walk to town to buy a newspaper and freshly baked croissants. The *Herald Tribune* isn't available on Sundays, so I picked up the big Sunday edition of *Le Figaro* and dropped into the cathedral's morning service. It was filled to capacity with many standing on the sides and at the rear—townspeople of all ages. Whoever says the church is dying in France has not been to Lectoure on Sunday morning.

We decided to take a picnic lunch to La Romieu, a tiny village just a few miles to the northeast of Lectoure. A scenic route, the D-166, takes one through lovely rolling farmland.

Laura spotted a number of hawks of various sizes as we drove along, and we continued to see them throughout our stay. We infer from their presence that there must be enough small animals for them to eat despite the compulsion of French hunters to obliterate anything that moves.

As we drove along we suddenly saw an incredibly tall tower looking at first like a huge grain elevator rising straight out of the distant fields. Not a thing of great beauty when first observed, it turned out to be one of the two towers of the thirteenth-century Collegiate Church in La Romieu. Administered by a deacon and several cannons, the complex is designated in church hierarchy "Collégiale." Although we found the tower closed to tourists and missed what should be a fantastic view, we had the great pleasure of walking in the lovely Gothic cloister. Though weatherworn and partly damaged, it is still complete on all four sides, and the beauty of its delicately carved arches seems only to have been enhanced by the ravages of time. Planning a future sketch, I photographed the cloister, concentrating on the tracery of one of the few arches with its five-sided rosette still intact.

Two sides of the central square of the village are formed by ancient stone and timbered houses under which arcades provide shelter against sun or rain. As we were admiring the flowering rosemary planted around the arcade, we were approached by a woman who struck up a conversation about the curative values of the herb for enhancing the memory and increasing stamina and offered us a twig to take with us. When Laura said that she thought of the plant mainly as seasoning, the woman acknowledged that perhaps there are some who use it in cooking!

The sun was bright enough for us to picnic on a small

grassy plot just outside the main part of town in the company of a friendly, furry mutt. One of the principal pleasures of renting in rural France is the *"piquenique."* As always, shopping, especially in the outdoor markets, provides much of the fun. A variety of cheeses, a loaf of bread, stuffed hard-boiled eggs, olives, local sausage, tomatoes, fruit, and a bottle of red wine make the best picnic provender, as little or no preparation is needed.

We dined before the fire at home that evening on *Billi Bi*, pork roast, and roast potatoes cooked with herbs, shallots, garlic, and prunes (another local product grown in great quantities throughout the region). Prunes turn up in many Gascon dishes ranging from meat and poultry stews to such desserts as *pruneaux au vins.*

Week of October 12-18

Monday

St. Sernin
Toulouse

We walked up the hill and along the main street only to find nearly all the shops were closed. Past experience in other rural towns should have warned us that many small town shopkeepers who remain open on the weekend take their day off on Monday.

We continued our walk to the eastern end of town where the stately hospital is situated. Behind it in a secluded public park are the ruins of the Chateau d'Armagnac, for many years the residence of the counts of Armagnac. As noted in the chronology, the last of the counts, a megalomaniac tyrant, Jean V, ruled over a large domain until, in 1473, the town was captured by invading forces of the French monarch, Louis XI. Thus Armagnac lost its regional independence along with other regions that had capitulated to the central power in Paris.

Sojourn in Gascony

Nearly 200 years later during the Religious Wars the Protestant Duke de Montmorency was incarcerated in the chateau. Legend has it that several ladies of the town, wishing to help him escape, took him a cake inside of which a ladder made from their own long tresses was concealed. Because the ladder was far too short to reach the ground, the Duke's attempt to escape was thwarted, and he was recaptured. Soon afterward he was beheaded in Toulouse in 1632 while Cardinal Richelieu looked on.

In the afternoon, I worked on a painting of two of the oldest houses in Lectoure, which are on the rue Fontélie, just a block away from our front gate. They are right above La Fontaine Diane, a thirteenth-century fountain used by pilgrims to Saint Jacques de Compostela. The complex architectural detail and the mix of timber, brick, and stone in the walls of the two houses presented a daunting challenge.

For dinner we returned to the Hôtel de Bastard and had another extremely good meal at a fairly reasonable price. We looked again for the friendly cat we had met on our previous visit, but he did not appear. Sue and Laura are serious cat people. (*Telle mére telle fille.*) Though basically a dog person and somewhat less infatuated with cats, I have succumbed to feline wiles over the years. Now in Lectoure we have reluctantly come to realize that, because of the presence of the German Shepherd, Tequila, on our premises, this will be almost our first sojourn in France without being adopted by a cat.

In our previous houses cats have often taken up temporary residence. Sometimes, as in the case of Miaulement (the French word for meowing) who came to us in Seguret, the cat's owners had gone away leaving their pet homeless. Other cats, such as Sophie in Saumane, were strays. It turned out that Sophie was a pregnant adolescent who bore her kittens not long after our departure. We had arranged for our genial cleaning woman to take her, and we received a note at Christmas saying that "Sophie a fait trois bébés." Having a cat to look after makes us feel wanted and adds greatly to our enjoyment of our temporary quarters.

Tuesday

Morning fog and clouds gave way to partial sunshine. We took ourselves to Fleurance, a town slightly larger than Lectoure about eight miles to the south. It was market day in Fleurance, which boasts one of the most impressive and well-preserved market halls in the area. The market square lies at the center of town surrounded on three sides by covered arcades. Close by is the 15th century mostly Gothic church of St. Laurent. Fleurance is one of the hundreds of former fortified towns or bastides still standing from among some 1,000 that existed by the end of the fourteenth century.

During the 300 years from the twelfth to the fifteenth century when the English, who controlled Aquitaine, were fighting the French, who held lands to the north, each side built these walled towns to provide security for the communities under their protection. They were sponsored sometimes by local nobility, sometimes by a powerful bishop, and sometimes by both. Today one finds *bastides* built by the English interspersed with those built by the French monarchists and the counts of Languedoc.

Called "new towns" when they were built, the *bastides* shared many common physical features, including a central market square, a church, sometimes a chateau of the local nobleman or bishop, outer fortifications, and always a rigid grid pattern for the layout of the streets. Usually the *bastides* were square, but occasionally, as in the rare case of Fourcès described below, they were round. Farmers living in town tilled their fields beyond the walls. In times of war, which were almost incessant, the towns became bastions against enemy invaders.

During the 14th century the French tried to regain the territories lost to the English. In 1328 on the death of the French king, Charles IV, Edward III of England asserted that he had a more valid claim to the French throne than Charles IV's cousin, Philippe de Valois. Philippe was nevertheless crowned, and Edward invaded with the intention of taking the whole French kingdom. The English were on their way to routing the French when the bubonic plague ravaged the ranks of fighting men on both sides. At the Treaty of Bretigny in 1360 (see chronology) Edward renounced his claim to the throne but was ceded more lands in Aquitaine.

We took a short stroll around the town, purchased scallops, red onions, some wonderful salad greens, and fruits before driving home. The afternoon was quiet. Dinner at home featured Scallops Gascons.

Scallops Gascons

Ingredients:
- 1 lb scallops
- 1 T chopped onions
- 1/2 lb fresh button mushrooms
- 1/8 cup white wine
- salt and pepper
- 1 1/2 teaspoons minced fresh oregano or, 1/2 teaspoon dried
- 5 T butter
- 1 T dried cèpes soaked in 1/2 cup warm water, reserve this flavorful liquid from soaking for use in the sauce
- 2 tomatoes (peeled, seeded, and chopped)
- 1 crushed garlic clove
- Parmesan, parsley
- toasted French bread slices on bottom of a shallow, medium-sized dish

Sauté fresh mushrooms briefly in 2 T butter. Strain juices into small saucepan. Sauté scallops in 2 1/2 T butter with onion several minutes, until just cooked. Add juices to saucepan. Arrange mushrooms and scallops on bread slices in baking dish, adding liquid, if any, to saucepan.

Sauté the dried, soaked mushrooms in remaining butter. Add garlic, tomatoes, wine, oregano, salt and pepper. Sauté several minutes more and add to other ingredients, along with mushroom soaking liquid and mushroom, scallop sauté liquid- to saucepan.

Reduce combined liquids by half or until quite concentrated. Correct seasoning and pour over scallops. Sprinkle with parmesan cheese and parsley. Brown quickly under broiler or bake in oven. Serves 4.

Wednesday

We arose early in order to drive Laura to Toulouse airport. We took the D7 again and soaked up the beauty of the lovely country through which it passes until the hills give way to flat and less interesting terrain near Toulouse. We arrived at the airport with time to spare. After we said our farewells to Laura we took off for day's visit to Toulouse.

We were frustrated by a farmers' protest march that blocked the main road into the center of town. This was only the first of many signs of the bitter resentment felt by local farmers against the prospect of reduced subsidies. The strong French attachment to the land, their almost mystical belief in the nobility of *la France profonde*, has led to long-standing artificial support of farmers. The policy has helped preserve the agricultural base of the French economy and has enabled some individual farmers to hold on to the land of their forbears.

Toulouse is France's sixth largest city and is a longtime rival of the somewhat smaller Bordeaux. The mighty Garonne River provides a physical link between the two as well as substantial economic benefits for each. But Toulouse has developed mainly as an inland metropolis oriented toward the Mediterranean littoral and the cultural ways of Provence, while Bordeaux has flourished as a vital port on the Atlantic, and, in an earlier era, as a colonial stronghold of the English during their occupation of Aquitaine. Today each of these cities offers many attractions to a visitor. What little we saw of Toulouse whetted our appetite for more.

The Celts established a city called Tolosa, which was amicably transferred to Roman rule as early as 108 BC and prospered under the Pax Romana. (See chronology.) Some 500 years later the Visigoths drove out the Romans from this region, which they renamed Septimania. Toulouse became its capital. The Visigoths, in turn, were pushed south by the more warlike Franks. In A.D. 778 Charlemagne, seeking to bring into being his concept of an integrated France, created the duchy of Aquitaine and the county of Toulouse.

The counts of Toulouse, reigning over an increasingly wealthy and expanding domain, considered themselves superior to the northern "barbarian" overlords and were unwilling to honor their allegiance to the French monarch. Raymond IV, perhaps the most illustrious of the Counts of Toulouse, had become one of the richest and most powerful members of European nobility by the end of his life. He died in 1105 while on a crusade in the Holy Land.

The Museum Saint Raymond, not named for the ruling counts but for an eleventh-century saint, was the place we chose to spend most of our time. Housed in an imposing mansion facing a charming square, it is a treasure trove of pre-Roman, Roman, and medieval antiquities. A special show on display during our visit featured busts of Roman emperors and their families throughout the period of Roman rule of Gaul.

A few steps from the museum is the Basilique St. Sernin, the largest Romanesque edifice in France and once an abbey church. The saint for whom it was named was the first bishop of Toulouse, a martyr dragged to his death by a bull in A.D. 250. Like nearly all other structures in the city, St. Sernin is built of brick that, with age, has mellowed into a soft rose to mauve color depending on the light. Brick made from the abundant alluvial clay of the Garonne is the only local building material, and it gives Toulouse its singular cachet. The Roman walls of brick surrounding the center city are still very much in evidence.

Construction of the basilica began in about 1075 and was completed about one hundred years later. A massive, ornate structure, it is most celebrated for its steeple, which rises to great height in five stages over the crossing at the transept. The dark interior is remarkable for the forest of pillars standing between five separate aisles.

After our morning of sightseeing, we walked to the center of town in search of a restaurant for lunch. We finally settled on La Frégate, which served a very good but expensive luncheon. The decor of the dining room on the third floor is elegant and appealing.

We dined quietly at home, sadly missing Laura. Sue made one of our favorite onion dishes, cutting the following recipe in half.

Onion Gratin with Gruyère Toasts

Ingredients:
3 T olive oil
3 T sherry or Armagnac
3 1/2 T flour
2 cups beef broth
18 1/4"-thick slices French bread
1 1/2 cup grated Gruyère cheese
4 lbs onions halved and sliced thin
4 T butter
1 teaspoon fresh thyme
2 T Dijon mustard

Cook onions in olive oil 20-30 minutes. Season with salt and pepper, stirring frequently until golden. Add sherry and cook and stir until almost all liquid is evaporated.

Melt 2 T of the butter in saucepan, add flour and thyme and cook, whisking for 3 minutes. Remove from heat, whisk in the mustard. combine onions and sauce and spread in buttered 14-15" oval gratin dish (or 2 qt. shallow baking dish). Butter one side of each bread slice with remaining butter and arrange slices over the onion mixture, buttered sides up and overlapping slightly. Bake in middle of 425° oven 10 to 15 minutes until bread is golden. Sprinkle Gruyère over toasts and bake for 5 minutes or more until cheese melts and bubbles. Serves 6 as first course or 8-10 as side dish.

Thursday

We packed a picnic lunch for a visit to Larresingle, another fortified medieval village just west of Condom on the D15. Built as a stronghold of the bishops of Condom in the thirteenth century, the town has been brought back to life as a haven for artists, craftspeople, and others who wish to live amid the reminders of an ancient past. The population numbers all of 138. Most of the houses are restorations of dwellings originally built into the town's wall. Little gardens in front of the houses abut the town square while rear windows look out on the open spaces surrounding the town.

In the center of the square are a charming Romanesque chapel and the ruins of the Bishop's palace. A moat (now grass-covered), drawbridge, and dungeon add credence to the legend that the bishops used this site to safeguard their visitors against whatever unfriendly forces might be on the rampage. We ate our picnic in nearly deserted car park looking out over moat and fields.

Again I took photos to be used as the basis for a future painting. I sketched the fortified bridge over the grass-covered moat with the tall crenelated tower from which ancient warriors would have had a commanding view of the terrain they sought to secure. Deep shadows contrast sharply with the old sun-drenched stonework.

For dinner we drove south about a half hour to Auch where we had reservations at the Hôtel de France, a restaurant made famous by André Daguin, one of the leading figures in French gastronomy and a major force in the principal trade association of French chefs. Although we had been warned that a reservation would be necessary weeks in advance, on entering the immense dining room we found that only two other tables were occupied. As is his custom, Mr. Daguin presented his large athletic frame at our table to discuss what we might choose for dinner. He proved to be a jovial host and seemed to understand our desire for a limited number of courses and small portions. Upon determining that we liked dishes from both *"terre et mer,"* he suggested that we start with fish and have a *magret de canard* as our main course. The *magrets* or *maigrets*, as they are sometimes called, are a kind of duck "steak."

The beautifully presented salmon and wild mushroom entree was accompanied by a delicate sauce. To our amazement the main course came in the form of a huge casserole covered by a rock-salt crust that looked big enough to serve ten. But inside, after removal of the crust, was a small breast of duck. In the fashion initiated by Mr. Daguin the duck was served very rare, too rare in fact for Sue's taste but just right for mine. Dessert was beautiful and delicious—four types of chocolate on plates were decorated with a filigree of chocolate sauce.

Aside from the high price, which we had expected, our main objection to the dinner was the excess of serving personnel who, because they were not otherwise occupied, hovered over us too intently. We decided on the basis of this experience that we prefer dining in less pretentious surroundings and that the absence of a guide-book star can be a blessing not only for the pocketbook but also as a harbinger of a relaxed atmosphere.

Our view on the subject of French restaurant classification was substantiated in a recent issue of *La Varenne* newsletter. An article cites British travel writer Richard Binns, who blasts Michelin's red guides for placing too much emphasis on ambiance and ostentation and the extravagances that drive up costs without affecting the quality of the cuisine. Binns tells his readers that usually they will get more for their money and a more agreeable dining experience by frequenting restaurants that have not achieved the highest ratings.

Friday

The rainy day allowed me to work on one of my unfinished sketches. Gail Messiqua, a Parisian friend whom we had invited to stay with us will arrive tomorrow. She will take a train to Agen and then a connecting bus to Lectoure.

Gail is a very dear friend who grew up next door to Sue on Long Island. She has often entertained us in her elegant apartment in Paris where she lives with her two teen-age daughters and leads a fascinating life based on a vast network of Parisian connections as well as ties to the American expatriate community. A blithe spirit of independent mind and will, she is great company as a house guest and is always ready to challenge conventional wisdom on topics of the day.

Saturday

At dusk we took a walk in town. First along the main path through the Maison de Retraite down to what once had been an extensive garden, now overgrown and sadly neglected. Thence along the road below the outer ramparts from which one looks south toward the Pyrénées. Despite the clear weather holding out all day and a lovely sunset, the Pyrénées remained invisible. Only a vague suggestion of mountains loomed on the horizon. Below the road are a series of carefully maintained kitchen gardens of local householders.

Gail's bus from Agen arrived exactly on time. French bus schedules are effectively synchronized with train timetables, and both forms of transport are very reliable. However Gail seemed not only glad to see us but vastly relieved that her journey was ended. The bus driver had been something of a madman—constantly conversing with the passengers, gesticulating to reinforce a running commentary on sights along the route and swerving around corners at breakneck speed. After retrieving her luggage from the bus we drove her slowly and cautiously on a little orientation trip around Lectoure. She had heard quite a bit about the area and seemed eager to visit nearby *bastides* and other sites. We dined at home by the fire that was needed more for atmosphere than warmth. For dessert, Sue served a lemon souffle—she's been perfecting the recipe since she was twenty years old.

Lemon souffle (sans flour)

Ingredients:
4 egg yolks
2/3 cup sugar
grated rind and juice of 1 lemon
5 egg whites beaten stiff

Grease and sugar inside of souffle dish, beat yolks until thick and lemon-colored. Beat in sugar and lemon gradually. Cut and fold in egg whites. Bake in pan of hot water at 375° for 20 minutes. Serves 4. (Another favorite variation of this dessert is a Grand Marnier or Armagnac souffle, made by substituting the liqueur for some of the lemon juice and following basically the same procedure.)

Sunday

Bright sunshine lasted all day. We chose two sites for an outing—Larresingle for a return visit and Fourcès the English-built, round bastide. The picnic lunch featured what we have come to call the fin du monde or faim du monde sandwich. Our name for this concoction originated several years earlier when we went on an outing with Laura and a friend. When we unpacked our picnic lunch, it turned out that the main feature, this same sandwich, had not been packed. Sarah putting the best face on the situation said, "Ce n'est pas la fin du monde!" (It's not the end of the world.) Instantly we all recognized the unintended pun on la faim or hunger.

Brie Sandwich (la fin/faim du monde)

Ingredients:
1 baguette sliced lengthwise
1/4 cup olive oil, 2 cloves minced garlic
10 oz. sliced brie
1 cup shredded basil
3 T white wine
1 T pepper
3 T chives
1 1/2 cups shredded sorrel leaves or other herb

Sprinkle cut surfaces of baguette with oil and wine. Spread half of herbs and garlic on bottom half, and cheese in slices on top. Spread remaining herbs and garlic on brie. Put halves together, wrap in plastic, then in foil. Refrigerate with a weight on top 4-5 hours or overnight.

After our initial visit to Larresingle on an overcast day, it was a great joy to see it bathed in sunlight. The ancient wheat-brown stones assumed a warm mellow hue, and the battlements cast dramatic shadows on the moat covered with grass of brightest green. There was little sign of activity on the part of local residents, many of whom maintain their principal residence elsewhere.

Leaving Larresingle we drove north and west about twenty miles to another *bastide*, Fourcès, built by the English around 1279. One enters the village by a bridge over the Auzoue River. The center of the village consists of a circular plaza surrounded by ancient stone and timber houses. Flower boxes everywhere are filled with brilliant displays of red geraniums. The lower parts of the houses form an arcade that shelters pedestrians from the weather. We took a table at the nearly empty town café, observed the charming vista and revelled in the clear autumn sunshine. I was sent off to scout a suitable picnic site. Strict specifications laid down by Sue and Gail included picturesque surroundings, a combination of sun and shade, comfortable seating, and maximum privacy.

All these conditions were met in the site we selected just outside the town walls. Here we looked out on the backs of houses that formed part of the ramparts, their luxuriant flower and kitchen gardens, a handsome stone tower over an arched portal, and, not far to our rear, a small stream. Barnyard hens cackled in the distance, delighting Gail, who has an inexplicable passion for chickens.

Later I made two oil paintings based on photos of the view of Fourcès from our picnic site. The two photos were taken from only slightly different angles, and each focuses on the old stone tower. The cloud formations changed dramatically within the brief interval of our picnic and we were lucky not to have been threatened by rain.

For dinner Gail had invited us to try a restaurant, Le Vieux Perron, in Terraube, a tiny hill town near Lectoure.

This enticing little fortified village is too small to be even mentioned in many guide books. It has several attractive houses and a thirteenth-century chateau, much restored during the sixteenth, seventeenth, and eighteenth centuries. The restaurant had been recommended by Parisian friends of Gail's who summer nearby and know the owners very well.

On the strength of this connection the owners took our reservation for Sunday night dinner even though they serve only mid-day meals on weekends during the off season. Thus we were the sole diners in an upstairs dining room. There was no menu, but we could not have asked for a more enjoyable supper, simple yet elegant. A hearty vegetable soup, *garbure* featuring beans, garlic, other vegetables and sausage, was followed by a *confit* of duck, and a pastry filled with custard. The owner served us himself, commenting on the house specialties and advising on the wines, two half-bottles, one red (a Madiran) and one white. The tab was modest.

Week of October 19-25

Monday

Our first stop was a desk in the Office du Tourisme next to the cathedral. This was the desk for the Syndicat National de Chemin-de-Fer (SNCF), ticket agent for the railroads where Gail needed to buy her return ticket. On leaving Paris she had mistakenly assumed that she could buy her ticket on the train as in earlier days. Not so any more. She was charged an exorbitant penalty for failing to purchase her ticket in advance. Afterward we headed to a nearby town, St. Clar.

St. Clar is a well-preserved little hilltop *bastide* built by the English in 1274. It is remarkable in that it boasts two arcaded central squares—Place de la République and Place de la Mairie. The latter has a splendid wooden covered market dating from the thirteenth century. The town remains an important agricultural center sometimes called Gascony's Capital of Garlic. However, since today was Monday everything was closed except for a hardware store and one *patisserie* from which we acquired some *tartes* for dinner. In the town many houses, though in good repair, seemed unoccupied. We walked beyond the walls along an inviting path that looked down on the plowed fields and across to distant hills.

Later, Astrid told us that St. Clar is a prime example of the depopulation of provincial towns. Despite subsidies and long-standing efforts to encourage farmers to remain on their land, the general exodus from rural communities continues. Many once-thriving economic centers are beginning to resemble the ghost towns of America's West. One of the few developments that helps support some of the more attractive provincial towns is the growth in the number of second homes bought and renovated by city dwellers. But they occupy their country houses only on holidays or weekends and leave something of a void when they depart.

On leaving St. Clar, we drove Gail to her bus stop. During the rainy afternoon I painted while Sue prepared a ratatouille quiche for dinner.

Ratatouille Quiche

Ingredients:
- 1 1/2 lbs tomatoes (peeled, seeded, chopped) or canned
- 1 chopped onion
- 2 minced garlic cloves
- 1 small eggplant cut into strips
- 2 zucchini cut into strips
- 1/2 cup pitted and chopped black oil-cured Greek or Nicoise-type olives
- olive oil
- 6 - 8 ounces Gruyère cheese sliced thin
- A few sprigs of rosemary and thyme chopped fine may be added

Cook onions in 2 T olive oil until soft. Add tomatoes, garlic, herbs, salt and pepper, and cook, stirring until thickened. In another skillet cook eggplant in 2 T olive oil until brown and not too soft. Remove. Cook zucchini the same.

Line pie or tart pan with pie crust, line crust with foil weighted down with raw rice or pastry weights. Bake at 450° for ten minutes without browning. Spread thin slices of Gruyère on bottom. Spread tomatoes next, then eggplant, then zucchini. Mix custard (2 eggs, 1 cup cream, nutmeg, salt and pepper.) Pour over vegetables and cook 25-30 minutes at 350°. Serves 6.

Tuesday

Blue skies and sunshine greeted us as we woke.

Our main outing today was to be a visit to Nérac, a historic and once very important town about an hour's drive north of Lectoure. It exercised its greatest influence in the sixteenth century. Initially Nérac was the capital of the small and relatively insignificant domain of Albret, but the rulers of Albret managed a series of prudent marriages, which brought them into control of an ever-expanding territory. As noted in the chronology, Henri d'Albret married Marguerite d'Angoulême, (Margaret of Navarre) sister of the French king, François I in 1572. Under their rule Nérac became a major center for artistic and literary development. Marguerite is credited as the author of The Heptameron, a collection of mildly bawdy stories with a decidedly anticlerical slant.

The highly intellectual tone of the court of Albret fostered the religious reform culminating in zealous Protestant opposition to Catholicism. Marguerite and Henri's daughter Jeanne became a fanatic in her crusade to rid her dominions of all vestiges of Catholicism. Troops owing allegiance to her defeated the forces of the French monarch, Charles IX, in recapturing the city of Pau in the southern part of Jeanne's realm. Jeanne promoted Huguenots to positions of power throughout Gascony.

In another move to extend the influence of this remarkable family Jeanne arranged the extraordinary marriage of her son Henri, raised as a committed Protestant, to Marguerite de Valois, sister of the French king and daughter of the fanatical anti-Protestant, Catherine de Medici. The fact that these two strong-willed women negotiated such a marriage of convenience completely contravening their religious commitments

Nérac Chateau d'Albret

shows how driven they were by the lust for power.

In Paris in 1572 Jeanne died suddenly while acquiring her wardrobe for her son's wedding. Thus she was unable to savor the fruit of her ambitious scheming when eventually, in 1589, her son ascended the French throne as Henri IV. We can only guess how she would have reacted when Henri, abandoning his family's strong Protestant tradition, uttered the famous line, "Paris is worth a mass."

In fact, Henri's renunciation of Protestantism scarcely pricked his conscience. He had actually abandoned his so-called faith once before—just long enough to avoid being killed in the St. Bartholomew's Eve Massacre that his mother-in-law, Catherine, had orchestrated while he was in Paris for his wedding.

His cavalier view of religion allowed Henri IV to carry on a remarkable series of affairs with women of all ages and stations. Henri's amorous proclivities first came to light when, at age nineteen, he seduced a young girl of sixteen named Fleurette. She drowned herself when he abandoned her after a short dalliance. A lovely monument erected in her memory is located in a grotto in the Promenade de la Garenne bearing the inscription "To that love she gave her life; Prince Henry gave it but a day."

Henry IV's reputation for womanizing did not prevent him from becoming one of the most popular monarchs ever to reign in France. He was greatly admired for his conviviality, his love of good food and wine, and his lack of affectation. It was Henri IV who declared his ambition for France was simply "a chicken in every pot."

We walked along the promenade by the Baise river admiring the 100-year-old chestnut and elm trees growing along its banks. The old part of town (Petit Nérac) is far more appealing than the newer part. The bridge joining the two offers spectacular views of the surrounding countryside. In the section built in the nineteenth century, the main attraction is the Renaissance chateau whose construction was finished by Jeanne d'Albret. The only wing of the original chateau that still remains standing houses a museum devoted mainly to the Roman period. Though the chateau was closed to visitors today, we counted our afternoon in Nérac well spent.

Among the many photos we took of Nérac was a view of the River Baise showing the old stone bridge that still connects the two parts of town. The trees on the left side cast dramatic shadows stretching across the water to the opposite bank. Later I chose this view as the subject of another oil painting.

Taking the D-36 back towards Lectoure, we drove through lovely farming country where herds of cream-colored Charolais cattle grazed here and there on the hillsides. Many French farmers harvest their hay in the same round bales now widely used in the U.S. This technology calls for fewer workers than do older harvesting techniques and thus contributes to unemployment problems in rural France.

Sue first urged me to consider these bales as painting subjects some years ago, and I have been drawn to them wherever they appear, provided they are randomly spaced and not jammed together in straight rows. Also very paintable at this time of year in the south of France are the rows of tall Lombardy poplars whose leaves are turning a range of brilliant yellows.

About halfway along the route in the small village of Francescas we spotted a hotel-restaurant recommended by

Astrid called Le Relais de la Hire. We knew from the restrained elegance of its exterior that we should come back and try it for dinner. When we did the following day, it exceeded our highest expectations.

Wednesday

As we had planned, we set off to the South toward Pau. Somewhat comparable in size, historical significance and level of urbanity to Avignon, Pau has its own flair and sophistication without the signs of the tourist trade, which mar parts of Avignon. The center of the town occupies a spectacular site on a high cliff overlooking the Gave du Pau and the snow-covered Pyrénées, which seem almost within arm's reach. The mountains shield the city from cold winds. As British troops discovered during the Peninsular War, in which British forces under Wellington defeated Napoleon, the area has its own mild semitropical climate. Often it is cited in weather forecasts as the "warmest town in France today."

Pau had been the southern stronghold of the house of Albret. After Henri IV issued the Edict of Nantes in 1598, (see chronology). Pau became one of the largest Huguenot centers in France. Catholic forces, however, resumed persecution of Protestants after Henri's assassination in 1610. The oppression assumed an even more barbaric frenzy after revocation of the Edict of Nantes in 1685. The following century witnessed a greater degree of religious tolerance, but also saw the tremendous upheavals of the French Revolution and the Napoleonic wars.

Once the beauty of the landscape and the mild weather pattern in this area were discovered by the British military,

Pau began attracting a large British colony (about 3,000 permanent residents today) who set up their own social institutions, built imposing houses, and established a thriving fox hunt. The influx of the British kept growing until Queen Victoria made the Atlantic seaside resort of Biarritz the most popular location for escaping the harsh winters of England. Today Pau retains many signs of British influence including an imposing Anglican church, British shops, and bilingual shop-keepers.

We walked east along the Avenue Gaston Lacoste, which looks out over the mountains and found ourselves in the Parc Beaumont, which is beautifully planted with a great variety of semitropical trees and shrubs. A large Belle Epoque casino, slightly faded from its original splendor, evokes memories of a fashionable resort. We walked back to the center of town along the Boulevard des Pyrénées and, after sizing up several restaurant possibilities, selected a brasserie for lunch. The wind was a bit too brisk and the air too chilly for the picnic we had brought with us.

For dinner we drove back to Francescas and the Relais de la Hire, where we dined in an understated but elegant setting. Only two other couples came in, as this was an off-season weeknight. Prices were very moderate and the food was delicious. The service was first-class. This is exactly the kind of dining experience we treasure. I ordered one of my favorite dishes, rabbit. When in France, Sue usually experiments with various recipes and has come to prefer a rabbit casserole featuring prunes.

Rabbit Casserole Pruneaux

Ingredients:
One rabbit (about 3 lbs) cut in eight pieces
2 T unsweetened butter
2 T olive oil
1 large onion
peeled and sliced
4 large garlic cloves chopped
1 T fresh thyme leaves or 1 teaspoon dried
1 cup chicken stock
1/3 cup beef or chicken stock or canned broth
1/2 cup oil cured black olives pitted and chopped
3 T Dijon mustard
1 cup pitted prunes
1/2 cup Armagnac
2 T chopped parsley
salt and pepper

Preheat oven to 350°. Heat 2 T butter and 1 T olive oil in casserole dish; sauté rabbit pieces over medium heat until brown, sprinkling with pepper. Set aside. Add remaining butter and 1 T olive oil to casserole; add onions, olives, and garlic, and cook over medium-low heat about 15 minutes. Return rabbit pieces to casserole and stir gently to mix with onions; add the Armagnac, chicken and beef stocks, and salt. Bring to a boil before covering the casserole. Transfer it to the oven and bake for 45 minutes or until meat is tender. Remove rabbit pieces from casserole with slotted spoon and keep warm while leaving oven on. Place casserole over very low heat, add prunes and mustard. Season to taste, and return rabbit pieces to casserole, stirring gently. Transfer casserole to oven and bake uncovered about 10 minutes. Serve sprinkled with chopped parsley. Serves four.

Thursday

In the morning we took the car to Fleurance for servicing. While there we did a bit of marketing and explored some of the residential parts of town.

We spent the afternoon at home, Sue cooking and I painting. I wanted to capture the view from our little terrace looking over the stone wall topped by urns and old stone basins whose flowers were past their prime. The four cypress trees, the palm tree, and the red tile roofs in the middle distance convey the sense of the semi-Mediterranean climate zone. The Pyrénées had yet to reveal themselves on the distant horizon, and thus are not depicted in this sketch.

Dinner featured herb bread with cream cheese and smoked salmon, guinea-fowl (*pintade*), and wild mushrooms (*cèpes*). There may be no more wonderful aroma than that of fresh baked bread.

Herb Bread

Ingredients:
1 T dried yeast
1 teaspoon sugar
2 cups warm water
5 cups flour (unbleached)
1 T salt
3 T chopped parsley
1 T fresh thyme
1 T fresh chives
1 T fresh dill
2 cloves garlic minced
2 T minced onion
1 T olive oil.

Dissolve yeast and sugar in 1/4 cup of the water until it foams. In a bowl combine flour, salt, parsley, garlic, and onion. Add yeast mixture and remaining water. Mix well, add olive oil and knead for about 15 minutes. Mixer and dough hook can be used when available. Put in bowl, cover with plastic wrap and towel and let rise until double (45 min. to 1 hour). Remove, punch down, knead, and place in oiled loaf pans and bake at 420° for 10 minutes. Reduce to 375° and bake for another 25 minutes until crusty and golden brown. Makes 2 medium or 4 small loaves.

Friday

During a leisurely morning as we were enjoying our view to the south, suddenly the sight we had been waiting for since our arrival in Lectoure appeared, to our amazement. In a magnificent, almost surreal display, the snow-covered Pyrénées rose high into the clear blue sky. This view was all the more exciting and exhilarating after the spells of dismal weather we had experienced. I was inspired to paint the scene from our bedroom in the sketch entitled "On a Clear Day You Can See the Pyrénées." After about an hour the mountains again disappeared under their cloud cover, but we still treasure the brief moment when they presented themselves to us.

After lunch at home we took off to the northeast to Valence d'Agen, a *bastide* on the Garonne built in the thirteenth century that still retains a few of its ancient features. We saw nothing in the way of antiquities as we wound our way through the outskirts of town. Our objective was to see an exhibit of contemporary paintings organized by Galleries Bonscaray based mainly in Pau and Biarritz. The paintings, displayed somewhat haphazardly in part of a rather ordinary furniture store, ranged from works of highly talented artists to other pieces that bordered on high kitsch. The exhibit was primarily of representational paintings, and included only a couple of abstracts. We were interested to see the range of art being selected for presentation by a reputable gallery of the region.

Late in the afternoon we received a phone call from Mary Day, the charming and lively daughter of friends of ours. Mary and her friend Gordon were touring Europe on a Eurail pass with a friend. We had invited them to visit if they were anywhere in our vicinity. They were pursuing an ambitious itinerary, traveling from Spain to Italy, Switzerland, and Greece. We told them how to reach Lectoure via Agen and arranged to meet them the next day.

Saturday

Much of the morning was spent in a search for paintable landscapes in the rolling countryside between Lectoure and La Romieu. I took a number of photographs of farm houses, round hay bales, Charolais cattle and the yellowing Lombardy poplars. Later I executed an oil painting based on a composite of several of these photos typical of the country near Lectoure.

After lunch at home we drove to the bus stop to meet our houseguests. Much to our astonishment, when we approached the little glass-enclosed bus stop, we saw Mary kicking furiously at the nearby public telephone booth. She was, it turned out, liberating a woman who had been caught inside the booth when the door jammed. Thanks to Mary's fast reflexes, the captive woman was soon set free.

Following this bit of drama we took our visitors on a brief tour of our town during which they recounted their travels to date and their itinerary for the next several weeks. The scope of their travel plan left us breathless and a little envious of the youthful ambition that would make all this happen.

For dinner we all went to La Table des Cordeliers, a restaurant in Condom situated in the recently restored chapel of a twelfth-century convent. Jean-Louis Palladin of Washington's Watergate Restaurant had been the chef here some years ago. It had been highly praised by the same friends who had recommended the Hotel de Bastard. La

Table's excellent fare and service exceeded even our great expectations. The old chapel's arches and vaulted ceilings were dramatically highlighted by soft candlelight. Plenty of space separated all the tables.

Sunday

Because there were no markets open in nearby towns on Sunday, we took Mary and Gordon on a short tour of Fleurance. We were back home in time to make them a picnic lunch for the next leg of their journey. We were really sorry that they could not spend more time with us, but felt lucky to have caught a fleeting glimpse of them on their dash through Europe.

76 **Pleasures of the Palette**

Although we had had only a few tastes of *foie gras* on our various restaurant outings, we felt that we could not return to Washington without something to offer friends in the way of a culinary memento of Gascony. Astrid had a friend who sold *foie gras* packed in glass jars, and we procured one of these to take back. Only on the night of a dinner party after our return did Sue discover that we had purchased a whole cooked *foie*. (She had mistakenly assumed it was in the form of a paté.) A last-minute phone call to a nearby gourmet market produced preparation instructions and averted disaster.

The unique delicacy of fresh French *foie gras* is denied to American palates by federal regulation against its importation. However, recent years have witnessed a number of American efforts, especially in New York State, to produce the equivalent in the form of the liver of a hybrid duck fed on a select diet. American foie gras is improving steadily but still falls short of what Gascony has to offer. The preferred way to prepare fresh foie gras is to sauté it quickly over a high heat with no extra fat or oil, season lightly with salt and pepper and serve in thin slices on Melba toast or French bread. A similar approach can be taken in preparing and presenting imported foie gras that has been semicooked abroad to comply with American import regulations. This product is usually shipped in vacuum packs.

Fresh foie gras can be easily made into paté simply by following a recipe for chicken liver paté and adding Armagnac or brandy and extra herbs. If foie gras is precooked, add it to other ingredients after they have been simmered or sautéed.

Pâté

Ingredients:
8 ounces fresh fois gras or chicken livers
1/2 cup onion, chopped
1 clove garlic, minced
2 T butter or margarine
4 T Armagnac or brandy
1 T Dijon mustard
two or three sprigs of thyme and rosmary chopped
    fine or 1/2 teaspoon dried rosemary and
        1/2 teaspoon dried thyme
1/2 teaspoon freshly grated nutmeg
salt and pepper
1/3 cup walnuts or pistachios (optional)

    Melt butter, cook onion and garlic slowly until translucent, add sliced livers or fois gras and cook 2 to 3 minutes more. Add remaining ingredients and blend in food processor or blender. Add salt and pepper to taste. Add a few walnuts or pistachios if desired. Pack in small ramekins or terrine, cool, garnish with parsley and lemon, serve with thinly sliced, toasted French bread rounds or crackers.

Week of October 26

Monday

This was our last full day in Lectoure. We packed in the morning for an early getaway the following day. Afternoon was mainly devoted to a visit to Astrid's horse. Sue and Astrid had formed a great bond based partly on their common love of riding. The farm where Astrid boards her horse is just outside of Lectoure. We drove there in Astrid's little red car; Tequila the dog occupied much of the back seat. In the field near the stable were three mares with foals and a rather elderly stallion. We had a friendly visit with Astrid's handsome horse, a chestnut gelding, and took a walk in the woods where she usually rides. Masses of cyclamen were growing wild all over. We walked by the owner's house, a once rather grand edifice that now showed the effects of long neglect.

Tuesday

We got off to an early start on an all-day drive to Valençay where we had reserved a room for two nights at the highly recommended Hotel Espagne. Even though we traveled on minor roads much of the way we made good time.

The hotel has great charm; it is U-shaped, with guest suites occupying the wings and facing an inner courtyard. It is a short block away from the entrance to the Chateau Valençay, one of several sites we planned to visit. The town itself is a bit to the south and east of the Loire Valley but close enough to the five chateaux we hoped to see. The map shows the routes we traveled on our tour of these sites. At dinner in the first-rate hotel restaurant only a couple of other tables were occupied, as again it was mid-week in the off-season.

Wednesday

Our first stop today was to be Villandry, the last of the great Renaissance-style chateaux to be built on the banks of the Loire. Known especially for its fabulous grounds, it attracts many visitors to its vast gardens of ornamental boxwood designs, vegetables, and flowers. Villandry was built by Jean Le Breton, Finance Minister of François I. Aside from a dungeon and high crenelated tower it has none of the vestiges of feudal architecture found in most other Loire Valley chateaux. Construction was completed in 1536. By 1906 the cost of maintenance was prohibitive and the structure was on the point of being demolished. It was saved from the wrecking ball in that year by Joachim Carvallo, a Spaniard who was the grandfather of the current owner. Carvallo abandoned a promising career as a scientist to devote himself entirely to Villandry. He was chiefly responsible for the restoration and expansion of the gardens.

After returning to Washington we discovered that the large fortune required for acquiring, maintaining and restoring Villandry was that of Carvallo's wife, Anne Coleman of Pennsylvania. Through our old Washington friend, Francis Coleman, Anne Coleman's great nephew, we learned the intriguing story behind the marriage of the American heiress and the Spanish scientist. Anne Coleman, an exceptionally bright but rather dowdy graduate of Bryn Mawr, had decided that she wanted to become a doctor. Her family could not accept such an extreme break with the conventions of the day. Ultimately, however, they allowed her to pursue her wish, but with the remarkable proviso that she study outside of the United States. She attended the Sorbonne where she met a fellow student, Joachim Carvallo. After two years of medical school Anne married Carvallo and soon thereafter they acquired Villandry.

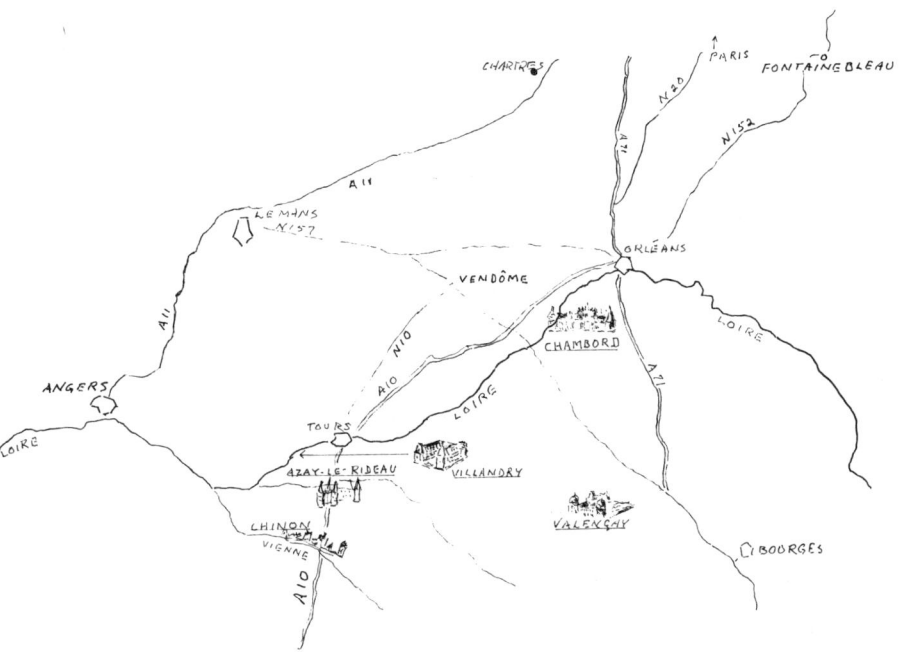

Before touring the gardens we guided ourselves through some of the principal spaces in the chateau whose paintings and furnishings reflect Carvallo's Spanish origins. The Goya school is heavily represented. We then saw an audiovisual show about the gardens, which is given in the first room of the painting gallery. For a magnificent view of the gardens and nearby countryside we climbed to the top of the tower. It was built over a twelfth-century keep, the only remaining portion of the castle that was destroyed to make way for the current structure. The tower provides the best view of the intricate boxwood topiary garden in which four square represent four variations on the theme of love. Depicted in a square dedicated to courtly love are the blades of daggers and swords used in duels over women. A square with four fans in the corner represents the inconstancy of emotions or "fickle love." "Tender love" is symbolized by hearts. The fourth square represents "crazed love."

The kitchen garden is laid out according to designs by monks in medieval abbeys who combined fruit and vegetable gardens with flower borders, especially roses. The shape of the cross repeated in many of the kitchen gardens reflects their monastic origins. Above the kitchen and flower gardens is a large water garden in the shape of a Louis XV mirror. From it flows a small canal that drains ultimately into the Loire.

These gardens make up the foreground of my sketch based on photos we took during our visit. The wet autumn had assured a luxuriant green in the plantings and distant trees along with plenty of color in the flower beds.

At lunch time we parked in an area overlooking the Loire valley and enjoyed the delicacies we had acquired for our picnic from shops near our hotel in Valençay. We regretted having too little time to spend at Villandry, but its extraordinary combination of high Renaissance architectural features and well-designed gardens that matched the period will long remain locked in our memories of favorite places.

From Villandry we headed towards Azay le Rideau, which is not far to the south but is reachable only by a circuitous route. Azay is situated on the Indres, a tributary of the Loire. Like so many of the other chateaux of the area, Azay was constructed by a great financier, Gilles Berthelot. But it was his wife who actually directed the work, just as Catherine Briçonnet, wife of the builder of Chenonceau, had supervised its construction. Built along the banks of the river, Azay brings to mind the nearby Chenonceau, though it is much smaller and, in our view, more appealing. After passing through many hands with the rise and fall of the fortunes of owners, Azay was acquired by the state in 1905.

First, we walked all the way around the chateau taking in its spectacular architecture, in which late Gothic blends with features of the Renaissance era. Built on the ruins of a feudal castle, it retains no visible features of the original structure. The principal feature of the interior is the great three-story *escalier d'honneur*.

The third site we had decided to visit today was Chinon, one of the oldest and most dramatic of all the Loire valley landmarks. Our drive west from Azay on another circuitous route took so long that we had time only to circle the town, pausing briefly at a couple of sites where one can glimpse the three separate strongholds that together form the elongated castle complex. It looms above a high embankment and looks down on the town of Chinon. A road far below the castle lined with ancient houses hugs the banks of the Vienne.

Chinon is best known as the site of the first encounter of Jeanne d'Arc and Charles VII who met in the great hall of the Chateau du Milieu, which was built from the eleventh to the fifteenth century. It was here in 1429 that the eighteen-year-old peasant girl had astounded a large assemblage of courtiers by identifying the Dauphin even though he had hidden among the throng.

Another great dinner was presented in the dining room of the Hôtel Espagne. Specialties of the restaurant are *escalope de foie gras de canard aux raisins* and *pigeon rôti á l'ail en chemise bombe talleyrand*. By the dessert course tonight, however, I could not finish the fabulous apple tart. Although we had heard that the institution of the doggie bag is unknown in France, we asked the amiable maitre 'd if he would be amenable to ordering a *"sac pour Fido."* He greeted the suggestion enthusiastically, while telling us how much he deplored the waste of food in French kitchens. We kept the foil-wrapped *sac* cool overnight on our window sill.

Thursday, October 29

We woke to the glorious sight of a beautiful blue sky that was to remain with us most of the morning. Our first stop after breakfast was the Chateau Valençay around the corner from our hotel. In fact, the proximity of the chateau was one of the main reasons we had selected this location for our brief visit to the Loire Valley. The fact that the chateau had been the residence of one of Sue's favorite historical figures, the Prince de Talleyrand, had removed any doubt about where we would stay.

On visiting the chateau today one feels the presence of this remarkable man as if he might still live there. Completely and lavishly furnished in Empire and Louis XVI styles, it evokes the memory of this wizard of finance, diplomacy, and the art of survival. Talleyrand, as minister of foreign affairs, had actually been ordered by Napoleon to acquire Valençay in 1803 for the principal purpose of entertaining foreign dignitaries. When Napoleon's ill-conceived intrigues in Spain led to the forced exile of the future King Ferdinand VII, Napoleon instructed Talleyrand to provide asylum for Ferdinand and his retinue who lived in the "gilded cage" of Valençay for six years. The chambers occupied by the Spanish royal exiles are prominent features of the chateau.

Only one other couple was on hand to take the guided tour given by a well-informed and charming young woman. She took us first through a long picture gallery hung with the portraits of Talleyrand's illustrious and noble ancestors. Other rooms contained many of Talleyrand's personal belongings, including much of his wardrobe, which was on display near his bedroom. Before leaving we had a quick glimpse of the large and beautifully maintained park with free ranging herds of deer, kangaroos, llamas, and exotic waterfowl.

We had planned this day to visit Chambord, which was more or less on our route towards Paris. In fact, neither one of us could recall whether we had visited Chambord before, but we had seen enough pictures to know that it would be massive. In that respect it certainly lived up to expectations. Everything about Chambord is outsize. It is by far the largest of the Loire Valley chateaux containing 440 rooms, 365 windows, 13 principal stairways and 70 secondary stairways for staff. The wall surrounding its grounds is 22 miles in circumference. Certainly it is grand, imposing, and as architecturally magnificent as one would expect from the mind of such inspirational sources as Leonardo da Vinci, who presented designs for some of the construction. But it is not exactly a welcoming edifice.

François I started work on the site of an earlier hunting lodge in 1526. He kept the project going, often employing more than 1800 workers even though the royal treasury was exhausted. François I refused to pay ransom for his two sons and looted the monasteries and churches to raise funds. He died before the work was finished, and it was only in 1539 that construction was completed under Henri II.

We walked around the grounds and into the tiny town of Chambord near the chateau. My sketch, which seeks to convey a sense of the vast scale and architectural clutter, features the chateau's reflections in the abutting lake.

Chambord was our last stop before the drive to Paris, thus marking the end of our sojourn in the countryside of France. We began the mental adjustment necessary to adapt from the leisurely tempo of rural life to the city's faster moving and sometimes frenetic pace. Much as we looked forward to immersing ourselves in the alluring ways of one of our favorite cities we were really sorry to bring this chapter to a close.

Our drive gave us time to reminisce about the three weeks in Lectoure. All of our sojourns have been distinctive—different places, different houses, different houseguests, different sight-seeing trips, and different cats. The memories of them all would blend into a hopeless haze were it not for Sue's diaries, my sketches, bulging photo albums and memoirs we have written for our children.

We feel that we have barely begun to know France, and could well be lured into trying any number of areas outside the southern tier we have favored until now. Moreover there are many other parts of the world we have yet to explore. But when we contemplate going abroad, France exerts a strong magnetic pull. The sights, scents, tastes, sounds and the French flair for living are hard to resist. Even though we are well into what the French call the *troisieme âge,* I'm glad to say that we still respond to the romance ever present in the French ambiance.

Though comparisons can be invidious, I think we would have to say that our time in Lectoure was the most enjoyable of all of our French sojourns. Perhaps it was a special sense of discovery, of finding places less frequented by American or other foreign tourists, and realizing that this part of France is unspoiled by the seekers after glitz and glamour. Lectoure and Gascony reinforced our appreciation for the simple pleasures of life in a small country town.

In Gascony we treasured the absence of the unattractive clutter that accompanies the tourist trade in some other areas we have visited. Preservation of the landscape, rural or urban, is dear to the hearts of most Frenchmen. But we felt that the citizens of the towns and villages in the southwest had been singularly successful in maintaining the beauty of both rural and urban landscapes.

Almost every day of our three-week stay seemed a distinctive and enchanting idyll, so that the entire time sped by almost too quickly. Only now, with the writing of these memoirs, have Sue and I been able to fully savor the rewards of each excursion along country roads, each picnic in just the right location, each restaurant with its own specialties and wines, each painting site with its call to be captured.

Astrid became our good friend and our counselor on all matters, big and small. Had it not been for her, we might have felt somewhat isolated and disconnected in our little enclave. We would have missed out on a number of interesting and enjoyable excursions. And it was Astrid who promised that on some rare occasions when the distant clouds lift on the southern horizon you can actually see the Pyrénées. That one shining moment is printed indelibly in our memories.

A Guide to Rental Housing in France

The following is a partial list of directories and other sources of information about house rental in France. The French Syndicats d'Initiative (Chambers of Commerce) can supply lists of rentals in their respective communities. One approach to renting in a particular region or community is to write the appropriate Syndicat, request their lists, choose a property, and negotiate dates etc. with the owner. Be aware that most French rentals do not include bed linens and towels, which must be rented separately. Ascertain the location of the places where this service is provided.

University alumni magazines, especially those of the larger Ivy League universities, often carry ads for overseas rentals of properties owned by alumni. Another periodical source is the *New York Review of Books*. 250 West 57th St., NYC 10107, Tel.(800) 829-5088.

Many of the following entries were taken from the March/April 1993 special supplement of *Travel Trade News* published by the French Government Tourist Office. (see below)

We have not included agencies that focus mainly on Parisian rentals. Most agencies make personal inspections of the properties they list.

AT HOME ABROAD
Sutton Town House, 405 East 56th St., 6-H, New York, N.Y. 10022, Tel. (212) 421-9165. Villa-vacation specialists. Apartments and châteaux in Provence, Riviera, Normandy, Dordogne.

BETTER HOMES & TRAVEL
13900 Fiji Way, Ste.113, Marina del Rey, CA 90292, Tel.(310) 821-9590, Apartment and villa rentals throughout France. Complete travel packages available.

CHEZ VOUS
220 Redwood Hwy, Ste 129, Mill Valley, CA 94941, Tel.(415) 331-2535, Country cottages, manors, farmhouses, villas, châteaux, and apartment rentals in Paris.

CUENDET PROPERTIES
300 President Ave., Providence, RI 02906, Tel. (401) 751-4978. Formerly specializing in Tuscany, now offering also upscale properties in Provence, Dordogne, Côte d'Azur, and Loire Valley. (This listing is not from the French government tourist office.)

EUROPA-LET
92 North Main, Ashland, OR 97520, Tel. (503) 482-5806, chalets in the French Alps, apartments in Paris and the Riviera, farmhouses and villas throughout France.

FAMILIES ABROAD
194 Riverside Dr., NYC 10025, Tel. (212) 787-2434. Sabbatical and vacation rentals, apartments, villas, and châteaux throughout France.

FOUR STAR LIVING
640 Fifth Ave, 5th fl, NYC 10019, Tel. (212) 518-3690. International real estate company renting, selling, and trading upscale villas, châteaux, condos throughout France.

FRANCE AMERIQUE
1560 Broadway, Ste. 511, NYC 10036-6902, Tel. (212) 221-6700. A weekly newspaper that carries housing advertisements.

FRENCH EMBASSY
The embassy refers inquiries on rentals to the French Government Tourist Office in New York. *FRANCE* Magazine, a quarterly published in English by the Embassy, is an attractive and informative journal distributed free upon request. Useful background information for travelers and renters. Write to *FRANCE* Magazine, Circulation Department, 4101 Reservoir Road, Washington, DC 20007.

FRENCH GOVERNMENT TOURIST OFFICE
628 Fifth Avenue, New York, N.Y. 10020-2452, Tel. (212) 757- 1125. Publishes the annual *France Discovery Guide*, featuring articles on points of interest throughout France and the quarterly supplement, *Insider's News*. Also publishes the *Special Supplement on Packages and Tours*, which includes a two-page list of rental agencies.

FRENCH HOME RENTALS
PO Box 82386, Portland, OR 97282, Tel. (503) 774-8977. Apartment and villa short-term rentals in Paris, Aquitaine, Dordogne, and Riviera. Offers cooking and French language class packages in southwestern France.

FRIENDS IN FRANCE
PO Box 1044, Rocky Hills, CT 06067, Tel. (203) 563-0195. Year-round homestay programs for houseguests in 40 homes—farmhouses to châteaux—located throughout the country. English is spoken in most homes.

GITES DE FRANCE
Gites are holiday homes (part of a house or an entire house) situated usually on farmland or in small villages. They are chartered by the company Gites de France, which sets the standards for this kind of operation. Some 36,000 homes, with about 170,000 beds, are listed. The accommodations are usually simple and prices at the low end of the scale. There are also 6,000 Gites-Chambres d'Hôte and 760 Gites Tables d'Hôte, which are equivalent to bed and breakfasts. For details contact: La Maison du Tourisme Vert, Federation Nationale des Gites Ruraux de France, 35, rue Godot-de-Mauroy, 75009, Paris, France. Tel. (1) 47 42 20 20.

HEAVEN ON EARTH
44 Kitty Hawk, Pittsford, NY 14534, Tel. (716) 381-7625. Personalized agency with approx. 750 rental properties throughout Paris, Riviera, Provence, and Dordogne.

HIDEAWAYS INT'L
PO Box 1270, 15 Goldsmith St., Littleton, MA 01460, Tel. (508) 486-8955 or (800) 843-8525. Paris apartments, intimate hotels, villas, country homes, farmhouses, and châteaux throughout France.

INTERHOME
124 Little Falls Rd., Fairfield, NJ 07004, Tel.(201) 882-6864. Approximately 9,000 listings—villas, chalets, and apartments—throughout France.

LYCEUM TOURS
9 Haddon Ave., Haddonfield, NJ 08033, Tel.(609) 795-9044 or (800) 257-7446. Villas to purchase or rent in La Croix, Valmer, Paris, and throughout France.

PRESTIGE VILLAS
PO Box 1046 Southport, CT 06940, Tel.(203) 254-1302 or (800) 336-0080. Personally selected villas along Côte d'Azur from Cap Ferrat to St. Tropez.

R.A.V.E. RENT A VACATION EVERYWHERE
383 Park Ave., Rochester, NY 14607, Tel. (716) 256-2676. Personalized villa, condo, and apartment rentals in France.

RENT A HOME INT'L
7200 34th Ave. NW, Seattle, WA 98117, Tel. (206) 789-9377 or (800) 488-RENT. Over 3,000 moderate-to-luxurious villas, châteaux, cottages, and apartments throughout France.

RIVIERA HOLIDAYS
31 Georgian La., Great Neck, NY 11024, Tel. (516) 487-8094. Specializes in apartments and villas on the Riviera and in Paris.

TAMSIN & COOKE
PO Box 8, Franklin Lakes, NJ 07417, Tel. (201) 337-6151. Large selection of villas w/pools on the Riviera, coast, and inland.

VACANCES PROVENCALES VACATIONS
729 Cutter Lane, Elk Grove Village, IL 60007, Tel. (708) 893-9402 or (800) 444-9402. Villas and country homes from simple to luxurious throughout France.

VACATION HOME RENTALS, WORLDWIDE
235 Kensington Ave., Norwood, NJ 07648, Tel. (201) 767-9393 or (800) NEED-A-VI. Deluxe villa, apartment, château, estate, and condo rentals in Paris, Riviera, and countryside.

VILLAS INT'L
605 Market St., Suite 510, San Francisco, CA 94105, Tel. (415) 281-0910 or (800) 221-2260. Over 4,000 villas, apartments, cottages, gites, and châteaux throughout France.

VILLAS OF DISTINCTION
PO Box 55, Armonk, NY 10504, Tel. (800) 289-0900 or (914) 273-3331. Villas. cottages, and châteaux in France's most famous resorts.